BAD IDEA

FROM THE SONNETS OF MICHAEL DRAYTON

BOOK TWO OF THE ENGLISH STRAIN

ROBERT SHEPPARD

KFS

Newton-le-Willows

Published in the United Kingdom in 2021
by The Knives Forks And Spoons Press,
51 Pipit Avenue,
Newton-le-Willows,
Merseyside,
WA12 9RG.

ISBN 978-1-912211-74-6

Acknowledgements

Some of these poems have appeared in the following publications:
*International Times, Lincoln Review, M58, Monitor: Global Intelligence
on Racism, Pages, Shearsman, Stride, Tears in the Fence, The
Abandoned Playground*.

Supported using public funding by
**ARTS COUNCIL
ENGLAND**
LOTTERY FUNDED

Contents

Bad Idea

Idea's Mirror

BAD IDEA

There is an ecology of bad ideas, just as there is an ecology of weeds, and it is characteristic of the system that basic error propagates itself. It branches out like a rooted parasite through the tissues of life, and everything gets into a rather peculiar mess.

– Gregory Bateson

Idea XXIV

I hear some say, 'This man is not in love.'
'What? can he love? a likely thing!' they say;
'Read but his verse, and it will easily prove.'
O judge not rashly, gentle Sir, I pray!
Because I trifle loosely in this sort,
As one that fain his sorrows would beguile.
You now suppose me all this time in sport,
And please yourself with this conceit the while.
Ye shallow censors, sometime see ye not
In greatest perils some men pleasant be?
Where fame by death is only to be got,
They resolute? So stands the case with me.
   Where other men in depth of passion cry,
   I laugh at Fortune, as in jest to die.

Michael Drayton

To the Reader of these Sonnets

I hear one shriek, 'He's no formal poet!
He can't *write*, rolling his pastry-prose through
white space into shapelets … Just look at it!'
You are too quick to judge, my english rose.
I hang out inside *these* sonnets, punching
echoes into new shape, because I take
poetry as the investigation
of complexity through the *means* of form.
You shallow censor, you'll hate these ones too.
From the depths of national despair, I roar,
gallows humour. I uncouple each 'I-
dea', bash my brains until opinion bleeds,
    interrupt the passionate civilities
    of Drayton's lines, until dying laughs.

(Overdub of Sonnet XXIV)

|

There's no muff too tuff for the Muff Diver
we discovered gouged on a South Downs bench,
wonder still at this self-advertising
copy, dangers of elect dogging paths.
I relate diving depths of human hearts
under rudderless swell of Brexit NEWS,
from melting Arctic to hot potato
Gibraltar, from brittle heatwave Britain
to the scattered shores of Lampedusa.
I'm no hero, can't even lug this mattress
up the stairs to cast you on, in your fresh
rôle as ideal lover, rolling over.
          My tedious travails need not restrain you:
          dive to the wreck of my pearly Victory.

II

Jihadi Ringo's fresh from beheadings!
Brexit means bringing back 'our' laws but not
our 'bad boys'; proxy executions in
the States will make us all accessory
to its law: Bring Back Hanging! Where's my proof?
It's swinging on the gallows of no-deal,
blood and drugs stockpiled! Moggy pledges his
Global Dividend in fifty short years!
But O look, look, I need enquire no further:
your mouth is foaming blood and Ringo's in
your heart, high on atrocity – no need
to convince me that I have hanged myself!
      States of Exception apply to us all,
      except to leeches, liars and lovers!

26th July 2018

III

My long division long lost in lost time,
I cross the cheque, cross-checking my love debts.
I subtract the cons from the pros and I'm
in the red, like the Brexit dividend.
Laptop up, I tot up this misery,
skimming the algorithmic nonconscious.
Griefs still multiply in this networked space,
filtered, decrypted, pattern-recognised.
Face to face, in ethical relation,
extortion impoverishes response:
we exchange our inflated no-deal rates;
you cook the books with lines I did not write.
      Take the lot! Leave me ruptured and bankrupt!
      Then I can't pay your Euro Divorce Bill!

August 2nd 2018

IV

His wit's only used to prove ambition,
a splinter in the hard heart of England.
Tautology's taught them identity:
Boris *is* Boris; Brexit *is* Brexit.
They don't say Racism *is* Racism
in Labour's pogroms and Tories' crusades!
He left the cabinet to sport himself,
and strives to entertain with racist words:
Look! Alien eyelids start and flicker,
the only life in a desert of cloth!
I used the 'post box' analogy first,
but not, I hope, as vile and vulgar 'wit'.
  Watch new facts blossom on his lap's laptop.
  Its scrotal heat will cool down his ardour!

August 9th 2018

V

given the histories of you and you

— Claudia Rankine

so, no to he and she and yes to they
Leave i to me or us or we or
Remain with I and It not I-and-Thou
he cries Peg the Pay of all below inflation
she says Leave I and I with them not us
I say I Leave. You lightly answer it
I say Remain it is not us and them 'our'
bosses' pay has risen faster than 'their' workers'
am i to say me no thing says as we?
they grab more me and press my yes to no
am I I if I delete my 'me's? who now or here
carves Take My Self it's never you or yours?
     let you and they remain with me or we:
     leave love to I and I and I engender it

15th August 2018

VI To Register a Life

Office girls paint their nails on the bus but
no poet sings them (except little me, of course!).
They'll be laid off (the poem must say) long before
their cremains will be popped in a casket! Too
much! Let's leave to perpetuity 'technical
instruments', when nothing shall remain.
Leavers' superfluous self-love will shade them
from the shame of our drugless almshouses!
Schoolgirls saunter towards their exam results,
happy to have learnt British history at last.
They weep that they didn't live through war's glory;
they hope for a piece of the action next time.

> Today, I lift you from the life you led
> into the eternity of your date of birth.

(in memory of my mother)

VII

In her scramble for African trade, May
plays the Commonwealth card! She dances big-bottomed,
begs prodigal children to come home to the orphanage.
They want London to stop laundering the stolen millions.
Abob in English Channel, drunken Brexit sailors
wield Gumboot Diplomacy in the Scallop Wars.
With battering-ram boats and stinging stones,
they wallop the French, quaffing carouses in wine.
Bo, in his cups, overcome with foul excess,
plays a swaggering ruffian at his constituency fête.
He steals a plastic sword from some blubbering kiddie
and stabs at a portrait of May: it buckles on the glass!
>   As this lot caper, on world and domestic stage, I wish
>   Keeley Hawes really was my home secretary!

30th August 2018

VIII

He can't take it with him when he's gone
but the funeral bill will make it look
that way. The leavers are leaving life:
the remainers must pick up the tab.
Through the loophole of language and down
the lift shaft of poetry, my old brain
drops two flights a second. My prostate
only leaves time for writing sonnets.
You're scouring your cheeks, scrubbing your chin.
'Stockpile pile ointment!' Brexiteers chant.
Stop! If *carpe diem* is warning
for the young, it's more so for the old:
  Trump must twitch his stormy Twitter thumbs.
  I must leave you these wordy remains.

IX Bo at The Oval

Not like other men, Bo muses giddy
metaphors of suicide pads and box,
as he strides to wicket to bat with wit
Eurocrats, remainers, PM (and wife).
The proles boo Bo, cry, 'He's a lunatic!'
They don't mean he has 'mental issues'; he's
a fat phallocrat with bulging ego,
entitled to titles, powered by lust.
Who can bring him back to our senses? (Wife?)
He rises – laurels wrap his troubled brain –
wills us to hate him, like Tiberius.
Cook's victory is read as Roman omen;
     he leaves the crease. Leaves Bo to fill the void
     Oval with his effortless afflatus.

X

Shall I compare thee to a Polish fitter,
sending our sterling home to his wife, who,
feeling frenzied hatred from our racists,
packs up his tools and moves to France? No.
That buggers up Drayton's sonnet with its
rich son losing his inheritance on
floozies. Perhaps I'm writing a pint-sized
Pound-Shop Post-Brexit *Poly-Olbion!*
Pull the other one! Every gift they'll waste,
fields of strawberries rotting on the stem.
They hate you, hate each other, and only
love this country as a false abstraction.
      Drayton loved a girl who didn't exist;
      she seemed like a good idea at the time.

XI

You're not alone when you take out a loan
or when you transpose my self into your being:
you a Brexit monad, me a digital nomad
whose algorithm predicts a rupture in common-
sense that threatens to translate subjectivation.
For the worse, maybe. But in this swap-shop love
we'll be absent to ourselves, lost in furtive spurts,
subject to visa checks at the Chequers border:
the uniform blue passport, the fixed biometrics.
What was mine alone sings in you as I bristle
with the collective: level applause for Corbyn's pitch.
You say: *I rather like that Jacob Rees-Mogg.*
     Disenchantment! I want my bits back.
     I'll loan out my own lyric intersubjectivity.

27th September 2018

Robert Sheppard

XII

Buffering on screen stops the mouths of Bo,
ringing round his warning, 'Don't Bottle Brexit,
you'll be paraded through Rome like Caracatus,'
a pause into which I drop my nine loose-leaf proofs:
contingency; precarity; heterogeneity;
intersubjectivity; outer-objectivity; transposition;
dissensus; interruption; and *multiform unfinish* …
just long enough to wordsmith an exemplar of the first:
'a speedy apprehension of thinking with the things',
before Bo unbuffers, resumes his several functions.
He earns £2,291 per hour for his damp stories
in the *Telegraph*, while speeding freedmen piss into
plastic bottles in the Amazon temple,
negative exemplar of the second …

4th October 2018

XIII

In these lines your words are scribbled over
but we can still see your Idea through the rust.
That scratched diamond is still worth pawning,
and your stained slips still Calvin Klein declare!
I'm drawing dirty pictures of your letters,
every bodily fluid ink, every body a script.
Under-read but written over,
every *sign* is your unfinished *sigh*.
Every body casts its shadow: spectral optics
slips one under every step she takes
dancing to the podium on conference speech day,
gluing her to every bad promise.
      May's Shadow wrong-foots her once more:
      some think it's Corbyn, but we know worse.

11th October 2018

XIV Presume Hot

Oh Peer Smut, you scraped under desk with your tool,
click-a-baiting; perjured, you had to go!
I greatly marvel that Hetero Sump still goes free
to lie and emote (plot and grope) around the Palace.
O! Hermes P. Rut of the dirty dozen, you
massaged our warnings (and underlings' things);
you brought us to life with sexed-up Brexit mouldings,
an old rheum's poet with his pother Muse.
I won't say Mesh Pouter wasn't asking for it,
but Hope's Muter breathed fire down *his* intern's blouse,
Ms. Purée Hot scorched with his hot suprême.
He stole from the Cabinet: Probity, Decency… His
home erupts with protest: 'It wasn't rape!'
He turns up the heat on *The Great Escape.*

18th October 2018

Fifteen

I thought 'Arcadia boss Sir Philip' meant
old Sidney, not Groper Green, snorting
desiccated hearts of his NDA
co-signatories up rolled notes (your pension!).
When Drayton writes of virgins marrying
at fifteen, it was a different world;
grubby men roamed the streets with bulky bags
of boiled sweets. (No, that was the seventies!)
Sheppard's recent sonnets (male, pale and stale!)
trope an NDA to air the rich deceit
of an embargoed Brexiteer (guess who!):
into the same then let the woman breathe.
      There's now no way to pay and make the 'problem
      go away'; data shadow falls on the receipt.

Robert Sheppard

XVI His Allusion to the Phœnix

You're bored by his allusion: a bird in fake flames
flaps in false equivalence,
like the Brexit 50p minting cut-price independence.
Your beauty must be clattering down his exchange
rates too. He negotiates with your Self, your sacred pyre,
causing a stink about your sovereign right
to burn up EU free movers. By the time
he gets to Phœnix you'll be rising, the latest star
to star in his starry story, to outshine and burn
forever! You kindle pyromantic futures:
Let's increase consumption as freedom nears;
they won't notice we're feeding them charcoal.
     A burnt-out Citroën on an M20 sliproad,
     his poem will leave you no-deal.

1st November 2018

XVII

The flux of time helps us to forget what was and what can be.

– Rosmarie Waldrop

Before it gets dark put the clocks back an hour
and in the morning put them forward again.

– Cliff Yates

I freeze the clocks in stopwatch Britain
to check out what might be or what might
still have been. I pass from age to age
gathering closer to reflective glass, breathing
'real wages, investment, ports, the Irish border'.
I huff on the mirror and mist it all
into a mystery: they never will have to have
been told, they'd never have had it so good.
Posterity will dictate prosperity: retail, services,
hospitality and (oh dear!) immigration. I
tell the nephews, 'Sorry about the directorships,'
but I've perfect knowledge
      of every economic forecast forecast.
      Grab the goods fresh or they'll perish the thought.

9th November 2018

Robert Sheppard

XVIII: To the Numbers (sonnet in π)

Everything, it seems, reduces to 'Parliamentary
arithmetic'. 1 woman makes the evens odd.
Even odder: 48 letters to Sir Graham could zero her.

(< 48% now rate the sum worthless.) Will Go

go? He struggles with calculation: why be 1 spare prick
at a dogging site while men aggregate like tariffs?
Only friction at the border trades them off. The 1
safe backstop is a tight buttplug!

My dear Idea, the singular Muse of these sonnets,

beyond division, you know there can be no 1 good Brexit:
there are only multiple bad ones. But enough about you!
News just in: Go is 'wrestling with his conscience'.
Lucky, says my Muse, to live in a time of resigned
selflessness. (List! Hear the latest: 'Go remains!')

10:03: 16/11/18

XIX

You cannot simply say leave. No deal! Know why?
There was a time once for give and take;
but now the research group with no research papers,
the bile of those who hop from hot to cold, stays.
Will you remain then? No! Not another plebiscite,
cracking its tattooed knuckles over representation.
No leave, no remain. What then *is* your question?
Love or hate? Try framing that on a ballot.
Impossible! all say. What next? Paradox as paradigm?
Yes and no, the eternal tautology? Yes:
a hovercraft rules the waves it barely fringes. No,
we're deceived by others', and our own, drifting certainties.
      'Love *and* remain … ' I think I've got you: then you say,
      'This year's word is *toxic*,' and you've lost me.

22nd November 2018

Robert Sheppard

XX

A nasty spectre, May's bitter Brexit plan,
haunts the glass towers of Europe, a flash
not in the pan (and not in the can). She tempts us
with classic British restraint, 'Mustn't grumble!' while
Rut misspeaks dead Leave slogans in his sleep.
He promised millions, migration curbs, unfettered control.
He's tormented by my sweet forecaster's downcast eyes.
He can't look her in the face as he denounces her: 'It won't
be *that* bad,' but she lays down the law of diminishing returns.
His resignation speech would be one long sigh:
'We voted for a future no one could deliver!'
She tempts him to jump off Westminster Bridge.
        The devil at the fiery border stamps his blue passport.
        My wicked smile sweetly gives way to 'Enjoy your stay!'

30th November 2018

XXI

She 'did hold up her clothes unto her navel before Mr Michael Drayton and … she clapt her hand on her privy part and said it was a sound and a good one, and that the said Mr Drayton did then also lay his hand upon it and stroked it and said that it was a good one'. Suspicion of Incontinency: London Consistory Court proceedings, 8th March 1627

The shitless scumbag Member, Rut, entreated his 'tart'
To a filing-cabinet knee-trembler and implored me
To draft his chat-up (as a sonnet)! I'd rather write
Amendments to May's doomed deal. (I did that too.)
With the same juggernaut passion he brought
To legislation and rural affairs of the heart,
I dashed off verses so ambiguous that even they
Might pass for a glittery Leave campaign jingle.
He whispered my dead droppings in her ears,
Like Cabinet ministers courting the shires. My line
About 'flipping your bag of British chips as you come'
Seemed to woo her. But she was secretly recording.
      He'll need more than the Attorney General's advice:
      No deal is good and 'no-deal' is worse.

Robert Sheppard

XXII: To Folly: State of the Union Address

With fools and Tories you can't go wrong,
when, honest people, your representatives,
older but no wiser since the plebiscite,
reject the only deal – and then reject the deal's dealer!
She *won* the vote, like the election before it,
but not their confidence: Bo juggles with our futures,
while Go dodges loyally through the dogging sites
where purest Brits spread their purist nonsense.
Theresa May wasn't born yesterday, but re-born;
travels today to Brussels, to tear open her raw stitches
for her Baby Brexit swaddled in the Union Flag.
It's Christmas soon: repeats of *Only Fools and Horses!*
  Let's sort out the racist bits from the funny ones,
  and stockpile them for Independence Day.

13th December 2018

XXIII

This should be a jocular rhyme in which Love,
banished Europe, in proud, privileged Britain,
is held in scorn, for calling a stupid woman 'woman';
he's begging – very fashionably – austerity's child.
In weeping Christmas charity I piteously feed him.
But, ungrateful wretch, he persuades me that Brexit
isn't our greatest threat. Beggars can't be choosers:
Labour's six tests will fail all ~~unlikely~~ *(del.)* events.
I dare call this stupid man 'stupid'. Once Austeriteers
control everything, they'll change everything – and
steal us away from ourselves. He'll be plodding with delegates'
consent as fleet desire melts into micro-fascism.

     He beggars belief: he whacks me round the head
     with a sock full of frozen sick, and steals my reason.

Robert Sheppard

'MAY ALBION NEVER LEARN'
– Charles Dickens

I hear some say, 'Corbyn's not in love
with Britain!' public opinion tickled by such trifles:
'He's been sent to Specsavers to look like Malcolm X!'
Read his speeches as proof. Judge his Brexit silence.
Meanwhile, Hunt is in Singapore, praising
the city-state that has 'no time for poetry', with its
extra fibre-optics options, as Grayling stays home
to defend his gridlocked railway 'network',
to hire a no-boats ferry firm for a no-deal Brexit.
Can't you see, in your pursuit of 'vital issues'
how these men imperil with their pleasantries?
They're resolute: their private dreams could be
      our public nightmare; Brexit is the sleep they nestle in.
      Where other men from depths of passion cry, you blink.

(Second Overdub of Sonnet XXIV)

2nd January 2019

XXV

Why doesn't Fritzy Foreigner relish English?
(Clodhopper! It's *lingua franca* at the EU!)
Surely, all my poems should *tsunami* the Rhine
Or avalanche the Pyrenees with yodelled felicities!
No, Brexit bonds wing them north to Caledonia,
To anglicise intricate *pibroch* on the *Orkadĕs*,
Warming the Arctic Puffin with my heated verse,
Melting the heart of winter ice with *duende*.
Bards on the Island of Ireland (and the rest of Ireland)
Hear me keen on your Brexit county boundary,
Hailing your stiff-necked loyalist with healing song,
Disarming with lyric the slaughtering *gallōglāch*!
 There shall my ballads be piped in unison
 To charm all the snakes in the greensward.

(for Karen Bradley, Secretary of State)

XXVI Despair

She ever hoped this land would never hate. Hope
crash landed on vain hopes in Never-Never Land.
No hope for the vote: hate elects despair. Rumoured,
never-certain votes are cast round ever-certain ears.
Uncertainty gives hope to both Brexit wings,
yet all hope's wings rest at the Kentish shore.
They flap like dropped order papers. If that
hopeless deal is un-dealt, then no-deal's the deal.
Abusers on the Green, buoyed by plebiscitic power,
hating hope, howl for free speech to call slaughter
on women representatives who refuse to be delegates.
Did analytics alone project fear on such despair?
  But then, today at least, her hopes lead to despair
  and not because they'll not be voted through.

(i.m. Jo Cox)

XXVII

... I fear these tory radicals these out of place patriots (or parrots) who
are so loud in their insults against the present ministry only want to make
paddles of the people to sail into their harbours of old sinecures ...
– John Clare

Do other nations face calamity like this?
(Several do.) Political virtue is lost with the vote.
That a sincerely held bad deal is put to death
by bad faith doesn't make it good, though Bo
asserts May is 'fortified by rejection'! These
islands sink under such mad amendments!
Can she return to Europe to express no deals
or no-deal? Or, with respect, to argue that Brexiters
love the country most? After 'one last heave',
are we to leave our father's imperial sins
to our sons' and daughters' remains? Or (as
Go says) shall we take back control of our fish?
      History (their logic runs) must be on their side,
      since you alone, on yours, violate their laws.

17th January 2019

Robert Sheppard

XXVIII

Who says Idea overrates her love of Europe? Bo!
He's sticking to his guns. Against these chaps who
think themselves smart with their memory phones,
he'll wave his battery of lines: he *never*
mentioned millions of migrating Turks. He *never*
promised piggybacking pay-backs and fuck-off pay-offs
or even dividends from Fox's phantom trade-deals!
They're all swallowed by exchange rates set by others.
That other lot haven't got a clue. They give their labour
and people like him gain thereby. He grabs everything.
Corbyn withdraws Labour from debate. 'So love,'
Bo says (at least in this poem), 'Don't ask
      what the White Male Euro-Symbolic can do for
      your subjectivity – ask what it can do for mine!'

25th January 2019

XXIX In the Zone: Out of my Senses

As rampant no-deal battered my heart I
summoned every amendment in my battery!
Should the tyrannous minority prevail with May
we'd see dogging sites clogged with lorry queues!
I see corrupt bodies bent open over bonnets, hear
grunts of withdrawal agreements, head deep in car boots.
I taste Brexit bile on a maiden's lips; she sniffs
the spiced-up tool of her next Kentish yeoman!
But when my part comes, to play with touching,
the soothing amendment to stop no-deal,
the sensual queen would offer keys to her truck,
tell the others to fuck off to France! I'd hope
     for aid from her. I'd get it: ZOPA, free trade.
     Even in fancy, I've betrayed my European Idea.

31st January 2019

Robert Sheppard

XXX Those priests which first the vestal fire begun

There's neither virgin nor sieve in Drayton's sonnet,
just yellow jacketed men in their fiery pomp,
flexing with ease into their celestial project:
solar panels to warm the goddess's hearth.
Here's Drayton's techie bit: mansplaining hands,
air carpentry, secret hydraulics of the shrine's
vessel scribbled in the margins of today's *The Sun*.
The men relax in the male same-old same-old.
Idea's eyes blink in this rage of history. Drayton's
thoughts are stoking themselves for pleasure:
he wants to taste her hot sauce on his fingers,
but his heart's a vassal to her Vesta. But smell the
      other *Vesta*, packs of desiccated curry stockpiled
      for no-deal! Let's put on the *mola salsa*!

7th February 2019

XXXI: Critical Mass

Imagine some capering ape trolling Idea,
leering over her profile like a Tory letch (one
safe from censure because they need his packhorse
vote). He scrolls my 'Bad Idea' post, texts *WTF?!*
I don't give one. I tell him: 'You're the interruption
that gives this poem form, your resentment its fuel,
as Drayton sheared his critics of sheer vigour,
weaned his wit with milk of their human unkindness!'
Since these sonnets are an impressive bundle,
though every Britpoet leaves rags to dry upon its frame,
why should *my* Idea be undraped like a dogger
in a Kentish logjam with this misanthropic mimic?
      Up in the air, I'm beyond measure. Below,
      the last bug terminates beneath the lorry treads.

14th February 2019

Robert Sheppard

XXXII Cry Me a River

The Arno's a low ditch, where Petrarch once
perched, though the Øresund, with no brag,
slips past islands in style. That wide boulevard
of imperial dream, the Danube, drifts from Buda
to Vienna. *This* is Idea's best history lesson, not
Moggy's lizardy lecture on concentration camps:
the Spree curls between bullet-pocked mirrors,
the crystal Seine shimmers, as his words slither on!
Idea sees Vltava's wine-bottle whirlpool waters
swell with global deluge (and plastic furniture) while
Amstel brims at the Dam, where beer embitters the Brits.
The Lee moulds Cork into little isles we British torched.
    By the Mersey's open mouth to the world,
    Idea sits in her Ladies' Day sick and weeps.

18-19th February 2019

XXXIII

His cloake of crafte, his doblett of desire,
… his Codpeece of conceite.

– Sir John Davies, *Gullinge Sonnets*

My eyes, brim-full with Idea's ripped jeans,
are mindful of an eyeful. In the head, in the dark,
the mind broods, and lusts to see for itself
the erupting soft flesh within each rip.
While the eye imagines a long tongue, moist,
washing over those island bulges, it's pulled away
from her plump pleasures. News just in: Article 50
may be extended to delay no-deal (or even Brexit)!
Idea shifts her denim on a barstool, eyes the TV, thinks:
I can see it all: he'll eye up Daniel's Delia *next,*
covet more sonnets to stockpile through this mess!
Our mutual minds see this heartless truth of poesis,
        the craving of art, the carving of artifice.
        Each rip in the fabric makes an eye for the mind.

Robert Sheppard

XXXIV

It's no wonder, Idea, that I admire your power,
ravishing the world with a single thought, like Dox
working round the clock to run it down, while Bo
buggered the Euro-bastards. Yet all I got was this lousy T-shirt.
Admire minister Fox's 'easy trade agreements',
'easy' because we already had them! You give head
to the wisest heads, that groan at no-deal. Go soils
Britannia's rustled bustle; yet all I've got is your lousy T-shirt.
No wonder you wouldn't want Codpiece Cox's job,
inventing new backstops in the deadlock, like a poet
squeezing a villanelle into a sonnet. Moggy purrs rhyme
in his own luxurious lap! All I've got is this lousy T-shirt.

     What surprises me most is that now nothing surprises,
     least of all, the weary slogan on this lousy T-shirt!

XXXV

Beyond belief! We watch leavers with remainers vote
no no-deal! A miracle maybe, but not consensus.
The lobbies are throbbing with selves. I flatter myself
I care more for Idea as idea than I do for my country.
She's dumb-struck; I can hardly lift a laptop to jot.
This chamber works well, but not to make decisions.
It expresses the wills of the People, the Parliament;
then whatever's left of Party and of Prime Minister.
My stitched-up eyes can't see the way until you shine.
I hear the commentary but not the debate until Idea
explains that May's last word tonight is to start again:
to bring her 'ideal' deal back until it's sealed with tears …

    Of boredom! My bad ideas are cured by Idea.
    My unclean thoughts extend past Article 50!

XXXVI

The PM, in blind faith, sticks to her sticks
but fails to stir Leavers or believers
to a chorus of *Land of Hype and Glory*, flies,
like Time, to the EU, against it, to conjure more:
'By hellish Bo, who swears against and spaffs upon;
By Gove, who thunders, Jove of the lorry park;
By the ERG's little list of traitors; by Moggy's notion
that Ireland is just a little nation (where he stashes dosh);
By little Bercow with his statute as old as Drayton's sonnets
(how dare he stop me asking again and again *and again*);
By all true Leavers who march, left in the mud by Farage;
By all wounds on the Remainer's rearing remains:
      I implore you to extend Article 50 by a quarter
      or I'll be named and shamed in Infernal Brexile!'

21st March 2019

XXXVII An Indicative Sonnet

Darkness summons the Tories: May may go!
Upon her leave, she commands their vote. But
Parliament ordains itself, slips away
with voting slips, votes (no); sleeps. Idea still
thinks the future transposes the present;
despite disjointed deadlines, timelines, we'll
return to Love. Bo leaves the room, smirking.
Oi! Night! you deliver each party its
love-nest downtime; why abuse me? I can't
remain Labour. I cannot leave either.
Whatever tomorrow bids, this weekend
I wish the clocks to go *back* to 19
      69: I'd be on TV again,
        courting a future different from today.

XXXVIII

Sitting late, Parliament bid PM to beg the EU stay,
or else we'll be unable to expedite exit. Francois,
the Bleeding Christ of Brexit, forgave, in spite:
'They know not what they do!' They do! Leavers
splutter splenetic, scorning remainer's remaining
arguments, pick over the remains of leave. None says:
You voted for pain; we'll deliver immiseration,
police at the ready for your retributive riots,
trained counsellors on hand for our no-deal dealers.
So now coy May approaches cool Corbyn,
but such late cosynchronisation seems untimely:
red lines ring under her eyes, not on his 'Marxist' lips.
　　　Reason, knocked back, remains out of sight.
　　　'Leave it to us' is a threat.

XXXIX

Francois, when in rhyme he quotes Bond's M,
leads the Spartan phalanx of 'perfidious' Albion
('on speed'), moves heaven (he calls) and earth (or hell).
That which *we* are, fated by fury to squeeze into a Trojan horse,
forced by May to spill out and seize fresh EU seats in May.
For the 27 granted her a Flexibrextension
to the Eve of the Day of the Dead. He cares not.
She's made weak by time and fate. By herself and *them* …
Spiteful Arlene, she frights me with her looks;
my manhood quakes at her foul backstop.
She comes to charm open an already shut door;
I fear the EU has bugged her hotel room. Francois bawls:
      'I come not in Hubris, but as your Nemesis.'
      Come to me, Idea, in your French maid's frillies!

Robert Sheppard

XL

The condition of his tenants and of his political party – he was a regular Kentish Tory – lay heavy on his mind. He spent hours every day in his study, doing the work of a land agent and a political whip, reading piles of reports and newspapers and agricultural treatises; and emerging for lunch with piles of letters in his hand, and that odd puzzled look in his good healthy face, that deep gash between his eyebrows, which my friend the mad-doctor calls the maniac-frown.

– Vernon Lee

Your wind-up Easter bunny taps across my desk,
Nodding as I hammer out my manifesto.
My ribcage rattles as though I were clockwork:
Hate is the fossil fuel of my polluted heart.
I bellow each bellicose belly-slapping belief,
Maundy money doled daily to the deserving *riche*.
While Labour's pains never cease, I'll profit.
Your moaning passion passes over my bloated pledge!
Leadership, Local, Euro, General – what election is it?
I've been up so late voting no to everything
My eyes are scorched with scoring zero. And who
Are you in bunny ears? Amber? Esther? Cinders? *Laura!*
     I'll just scroll through these endless death-threats
     And fling a few inflammatory *mots* into circulation.

Maundy Thursday 2019

XLI Love's Lunacy

Why do I speak of Remain or write of Leave
if every repeated word now fills me with horror,
when Haewei or Putin harvest my spluttered woes
and May's ministers leak like recycled nappies?
What's to say, or do, when Brextinction Rebels
glue themselves to May's every utterance?
Business as Usual is *Death!* That's a no-brainer,
now every loony signs up as Euro-Candidate!
But still distracted to distraction, I rail
against Idea's materialistic cartographies,
her postnational Euro-spatiality. First I call
her an utopian, then an atopian; now I'm lost for words.
        Only her echo remains; Next I'll curse her
        as a traitor; then I'll bless her little cotton socks!

25th April 2019

XLII The Michael Drayton Companion (1619)

When, by thy bright Ideas standing by,
I found it pure, and perfect poesy.

– Ben Jonson

Some like my multiform methods,
and commend my social poetics.
Some say I'm a funny old translator,
'expanded' like a supersized codpiece.
Some that I excel in explicit vitality.
But others call this strange ventriloquism
'unsuccessful and overheated, loud and repetitive.'
Ignore my grudge over the 'esquire' thing. Now
Duffy's off, poets leave the laureateship alone.
Am I not best remaining bard for Brexit's long betrayal,
the 'better spirit' that even Shakespeare envied,
before I drank him to death with fat Ben?
　　　　I'll knock one out for the local elections. Free.
　　　　Flick through the only Companion I need: you.

XLIII

Why should your fair eyes and soothing words
dispense such grace upon every acetic voluptuary,
while I crouch in the darkness of Euro-univeralism
and get no glancing postnational illumination?
No wandering star messes with Mallarmé's constellations,
or screams across the face of Gomringer's icons,
nor unsettles Adorno's negations of Old Europe's
fraudulent freedoms. O! Theory, join up the dots.
Oh, why does your beauty suggest a customs-union
as Labour's only way out of the European Union?
Let's not be as ignorant as at the last referendum,
but (please!) let the next be the last referendum!
     In this pause to think, I pause to think ill:
     how not to get the blues while singing the blues.

9th May 2019

XLIV

While my weekly sonnet should eternize Idea,
every daily Brexit debate is Time she won't get back!
She makes a map of my wrinkled misery, charts
our disgrace, to navigate the EU elections, the terrain
they dare to name 'a consequence-free environment'.
Tyrannising Time trips May's world-outwearying
span. Her fourth defeat shall be her final deal.
Then it'll be time for a last visa-free Euro recess:
British disdain amongst the scattered hegemonies.
But then: imagine Green youth returning rejuvenated
to remain and reform. Or: black age to leave, ruling
oppressive lines, to reproduce its repression eternally.
    I'll keep her, enfleshed in words, from Albion
    and its grave. My name will fuck hers forever!

16th May 2019

XLV

Ministers sadly sit outside May's bolted door,
yet she is deaf and will not hear their fears.
Leadsom drops her news, panting with passion.
Since May distains to talk to the swivel-eyed,
the meme from *Downfall* can't be re-mimed, yet.
She's assured that tenacity will be her legacy;
every defeated Tory in the EU poll will tug her hearse,
wherein the world will soon entomb her name.
Senseless West Kirby UKip I pointed and cried 'Fascist!'
Idea cannot admit pleasure until desire has played out
the crisis of the nation amid transnational Capital. Like
Orpheus I sing through the wood-wide-web, vote Green;
     Idea yells at Yaxley-Lennon strutting in Bootle.
     She's kinder to this fascist than, silent, she is to me!

23rd May 2019

Robert Sheppard

XLVI

Dirt-track empiricism splatters flash-blade expertise.
It simply follows simple evidently-true simplism,
sees clear what professors cannot, who track reason,
trail doubt, with their foreign talk of dissensual commons.
Each vile actor in this heinous leadership anointment
is brought blindfold to Thatcher's Tomb, to make the pledge.
If the hollow ground bubbles with blood he (or she) has it!
Will it be Bo or Go? Or Savvy Javid (The Baby-Faced
Baby Killer), Graab, 80%? Leader Leadsom or Pestilent Esther?
Not yet departed, May comes near, that raw ambition slew,
mute from her last EU summit: Brexit leads, matched by Remain.
Her ancestral Swiss-cheese wounds ooze wormy compromise.
    So what? I shout 'Hang her!' at the BBC News.
    It seems to help – but it'll only raise the dead.

(for Victor Merriman)

XLVII

Proud of his Tweets, Trump's
dumb thumbs pad school bully wit.
So long as there's credit on his phone
there are *MAGA* crowds to welcome him to London.
Protest? Paid actors acting out sad acts (like
Henslowe's men mincing my eternal lost lines)!
Tory pretenders tumble like clowns.
With no shouts or claps at every pause
between his stumbled words, he sits
scowling at empty applause. He will enter
this moment, buy transnational space
within 'our' national places.
      (The anthology misprints my chosen verb 'eternize'.
      A new word *enternizes* the world as I enter you!)

6th June 2019

Robert Sheppard

XLVIII Crackpot Caracatus

Stupid! I hate Bo, which I'd have him know,
but he'd not care. Naked ambition parades her winning looks
(draping her locks between the lights of his campaign car).
He cries: *Prorogue! Go's pawns bear fasces for Bo!*
Stands quivering like a scarecrow at Europe, the White
Coif of Dover (while littoral pleasures slip out below:
an undraped satyr thrusts in hatchback belly-wobble).
He hires himself another 'personal assistant',
acknowledges *her* bastard policies as his own:
I bring unity: 'our' uniformity will fit you all
(like scarlet corsets leaning back in leather seats;
you may sit by them and play with yourself).
  Don't say a word. Don't betray your old ways:
  When a woman says no-deal she means Deal!

XLIX

And Drayton's *justly sirnam'd Golden-mouth.*

– Everard Guilpin

Dense brain, censor in the head, retreats into
abstraction, but calls my lines 'abstract'. It could
take my poem's pulse but never feel passion
spark between sizzling limbs under searing rays.
My pen drags sonnets across this page, unlike
Bo's swift poison ejected in viperous spaff.
Nazanin's on hunger strike; he'll eat his words.
He's bleeding votes from parched Tories, as I write.
His throbbing index of intention pushes
up into their sitting down! At any moment:
any thing! Political subjects in mad,
blind, despised, and living kink, mute their own thoughts.
      Hear what post-European Idea opines.
      Then read – be appalled – don't just applaud – my lines!

20ᵗʰ June 2019

Robert Sheppard

L Sovereign Power

Across the Channel, in the remote countries,
a Sunday afternoon TV British pilot is tortured;
the 'Ode to Joy' piano-wire garrottes him!
Euro-lawyers are testing treaties on us, coolly.
It's their choice to *not* undo the deal, we say.
It's do or die, Bo says. Actually die. Boundless
Bo binds himself to pitchfork the Incubus
off his back, then staunch the bleeding.
They merely bleed the prisoner's corpse dry
and close up the festering wound of Europe.
It's so difficult to poeticise tarrifs and trade! At least
I'm not the only one with a kill-or-cure mistress
        flinging a laptop at the floor. All because the wine-
        stain on the sofa looks like a little map of England!

26th June 2019

LI

I recall the uncertain times through which
I've loved you, the unexpected ways they
(and you) have drawn me by resistless force
beyond prerogatives of dominance.
I'm amazed to witness: the fall of May,
her largesse in vain legacy follies;
fake news hi-tech for the Irish Border;
Farage's troops turning their backs like Nazis;
we and Europe pain ourselves to sever.
Now the Age of Immiseration burns
through reeling heat of the Anthropocene.
While Bo blows hot air, and Hunt hunts fox, I'm
      constant as a statue with a stiffie
      standing at the centre of thick traffic.

4th July 2019

LII

Bo! Will you cheat us of our vote, to take (back)
everything and never give us voice? Your eyes
charm the few to grant what you'll ever retain!
Try Trump-like tyrannical tirades against
Sir Kim before you're anointed: show
Eton's 'effortless superiority', this
chain that is round *us* now. I'm trying to laugh
but you're a piece of work! No talk of pity
in your optimistic phallic energy.
No proof of no-deal's no-strings-attached reward.
No one boasts now of the Brexit dividend.
Crank up your car strewn with old crackers, crisps, *Tin
Tin in the Congo* and *Britannia Unchained.*
Kick your can do down the rolling English road.

LIII Cry Me a River (2)

Coal smoke and Spring move down the
Brick-lined gas-lit streets on the
Chill wind from the Mersey…
It hasn't taken me long
To find the only place where
I will find friends in Europe.

– Kenneth Rexroth

Misty Mersey, over whose grey-green mudflats
my bountiful Idea bounces with gusto;
O estuary, where oily cormorants plunge
deep channels, Idea re-locates whiteness,
spectre in the spray. She empties national
identities. Across the water, waste wafts
from chimneys' flares; nightbirds gather to spend
white seed, impearled blossoms glistening in
nectar-dripping drizzle. Idea sips her gin.
If Shakespeare's dark lady was born a Sheppard,
then I would hope to hook more than a goldfish
hanging over these railings for her to pass.

> Liverpool, temper my art to your futures,
> and Mersey, anchor my heart to dispersal.

19th July 2019

Robert Sheppard

LIV

Enthusiasm is not integrity,
Hope is not knowledge.

– Kenneth Rexroth

Read of Booster Bo's elastic positions or
dreary abstracts of his head-butting no-deal;
there's no room for my interlineal jibes
now my best jokes have been reshuffled.
Elegies to my Muse's flexible citizenship
are penned in grinning grief, while Back Hand Polly
practises her noose, Graab grasps cross-channel traffic
at last, and Bo's chipped bust of Pericles (or is it Nero?)
is repositioned. Praise his pluck, his optimism, his spaffs
and gaffes, his threats, his offering of 'us'
to 'their' sacred project – though not too sacred to not
leave a job for his brother. They've left Leave behind.
        We're fucked, but it's only to be expected of a man
        who's '*literally* bursting with spunk'! Who says?

25th July 2019

LV

My fair, if you but register to vote, it
may speak volumes at the election.
There won't be a second referendum now –
except in Scotland, or in the North.
Booster Bo, turbocharged with active verbs, hoists
Manx kippers, kicks Welsh chicken, across
performative scripts for his 'Awesome Foursome'.
(Move Heaven, Earth, for revocation!)
Quarter my brain, see what I see: the sore rump
of Britain as a Gruesome Twosome,
sacrifice of countries already othered:
nationhood unthreads ethnicity.
      Governance of Earth where our two bodies melt
      in global heatwave registers now.

1st August 2019

LVI Doggerland

When like a dogger I found my love,
fingered through the open car window,
upon the bonnet I spread her out
to prove if she'd still be in demand
after Brexit. No sooner did blokes
in wormy delight unthread their threads,
show that this is our true National Sport,
voted boss by the brave mounting brood.
And when the spumes of sweet desire filled
the air, and Go's grove lay moist beneath
the spunky Brits, I proved that even
a no-deal leaves no-end of supply!
    Thus far from my non-exclusive breast
    her breasts bounce in self-sufficient flight.

8th August 2019

LVII

Bo can see it most clearly by not looking,
and yet it's there for all to see, in plain sight:
we're 'first in line' for American trade deals,
rich Empire hidden in his murky vitrine.
Idea likes the look of herself, fake natural,
out where the branches blossom with lingerie.
Her eyes flash in radiant fluxion: we are
becoming minor; she's becoming mirror.
Bo sees through the trance of his conjury
more than classical journalese could express.
Here's his better world that's pure idea, unseen:
'collaborators' distract us from its flame!
      Sonnets are too short to show us everything,
      lost in their own perfections, imperfectly.

LVIII

In former times, rich bastards
stockpiled during civil, or world, wars,
and waited until peacetime to buy up the bombsites cheap,
but now they bury treasure deep off-shore
to wait for *their* Brexit dividend. Greenland
may not be for sale but Britannia is. Dig
deep in your trouser pocket and hold your tool
while she plays alone with her rich beauties.
Nearer such men come, Idea farther flies off
into her privileged foreignness.
It's all the EU's fault that we want to leave,
Macron's and Merkel's and Murphy's.
          Why wouldn't Ireland want to hook itself up
          to a few last strands of our history and be done with it?

59 From the Proverbs

A Leaver remained just long enough at the Belve to quote his quota of quotes. I, a Remainer, on the verge of leaving, lurked awhile, amused.

They who are bursting with spunk, spend! spend! spend! he began.

Never play leapfrog with a Brexit unicorn, I warned.

The bonobos of Kent are wiser than the pandas of Parliament.

And he again: *They who suck the longest spout, spit the greatest seed!*

Every day has its dogging, I quipped; *Nobody is born with a backstop.*

She who hangs the most, pleasures the longest, he surmised.

Ah, says I: *Suicides in cells save judges much judgement.* So he: *The English were good*

when the laws were writ in good English. I ventured a prediction:

If the 'onboard entertainment' on the Glasgow Express turns out to be a gang of headbutting Brexit Party-goers then Scots are destined for independence. Then he:

Robert Sheppard

If all Leavers were laid end to end, Booster Bo would build a bridge of their bodies and trot across to Ulster on Incitatus.

I: *Labour is light where Lib Dems do pay.* He: *He who seeks to be Caretaker needs to take care!*

Light goods weigh heavy sent far, I tried, for trade. *Expert on exports!* he volleyed; *When Fortune calls, there's always a seat in the Lords.*

'Stop!' cried Idea, back from the bathroom and its mirror, 'You are both proven fools. There is only one big idea: the end of pure identity.'

LX

Define Bo's options. Powerless to go to
the country, he'll prorogue and purge more rebels,
declare his fate as extreme minority,
but cast his life story as Octavian's.
Let shouting 'Shit!' at PMQs be his shame;
let lounging Moggy be his lickspittle, so
we may read policy through their attitudes.
Compare their worth with others' brave excursions:
the single Tory crossing the tense chamber –
claps for Tan Dhesi's race demand, boos to Bo!
Tell me, has there been such a week in history:
the House is sitting; now the House is rising?
> *There are easier ways to govern a country.*
> *Even North Korea trades on WTO.*

5th September 2019

Robert Sheppard

LXI Since there's no help,
come let us kiss and part

There's no help: MPs pin Speaker to throne,
boo the Tories. They'll get no more sittings
despite the State of Exception, for Bo's
and the Cum's dirty algorithmic tricks
redact all the vows and votes of the House.
When they meet on the other side of Time
(for those rogues have prorogued the no-deal clock)
the 'boring' arguments will be the same!
Now at last gasp of Bo's majority,
with his plans failing, and with speechless wave,
he blossoms in untruth, though fenced in by
'events': protest, court action (and Farage).
      Idea has five weeks to polish her mirror;
      I have two more sonnets to polish her off.

12th September 2019

LXII

As Bo begins, he mostly ends:
his best show is non-appearance. Where
he is most deficient, votes, he mostly vetoes:
his best plans are silence. I dream of
marching against him, but my knee collapses;
the ice pack burns: I drown in dry despair.
Ravished by Idea, I can think it through
but cannot write it down – without her touch.
All I desire is embedded in her body
but her social imaginary is a project not a product.
I build my hopes a world above her utopic sky:
down below, her rabbit creeps into my mole hole.
     The press films Bo saying, 'The press isn't here!'
     The Father of Lies is fucking his Mother of Parliaments.

19th September 2019

LXIII

Parliamentary truce may not be called, Love,
simply because you have power of Prorogue.
Neither side escapes to post-Eurocentric
identities. Neither party wins the poll.
Bo is in New York! He trembles before Trump.
You are in old Brighton to deselect the
only MP to follow me on Twitter!
My heart craves the motion that we shall Remain.
These are the moments when the battle should pause,
yet the Cum's chaos gaming subverts the state.
Come, let's Labour-weekend at the Metropole,
knock out 'an exciting composite motion'!
      Let the world note my next sonnet is deferred,
      like your post-election Euro decision.

IDEA'S MIRROR

Amidst those shades wherein the Muses sit,
Thus to Idea, my Idea sings ...

– Michael Drayton

the same time is already history
without a mirror

– Tom Raworth

Idea 3, 1599

Many there be excelling in this kind,
Whose well trick'd rimes with all inuention swell,
Let each commend as best shall like his minde,
Some Sidney, Constable, some Daniell.
That thus theyr names familiarly I sing,
Let none think them disparaged to be,
Poore men with reuerence may speake of a King,
And so may these be spoken of by mee;
My wanton verse nere keepes one certaine stay,
But now, at hand; then, seekes inuention far,
And with each little motion runnes astray,
Wilde, madding, iocond, and irreguler;
Like me that lust, my honest merry rimes,
Nor care for Criticke, nor regard the times.

Michael Drayton

1

my interior eyes into myself I
see myself hopelessly creative help-
lessly critical heaving my breast
(in your future memory) my breathy song
quite a classy act for your seedy dive
damn the grim inevitability of Brexit ads (I
sing) the pure information they bestow on us
come admire my flashing love lights
on TV I see Bo's fearful outward eyes
as he resigned before he could be elected 'I
am not that person' appears all night in dreams
waffling distracted about a better world
lost in his show when he should show us us
I gainsay his gains and gain his loss as plus

2

Bo strives to entertain
his Brexit case with needy words
waltzing the Taoiseach around the Wirral where
wodwos await the worm on public footpaths
(obscure moist bridals) whispers vulgarisms
in the dark Spenserian tunnel of Anglo-
Irish exchange *Nothing Is True*
the election sorted though the common voice
(Pseudo-Murphy reminds him) elects Remain
Bo laughs and claps and slaps his jolly good non-
paper in his non-judgement non-delivers
virtues against which I sing resistance
against vulgarity I endeavour to become
one (of many) deserving of history

3

grave EU council assembles
to police by protocols its politics
Bo's glory springs from sovereign
view of self and state (his deal)
his loving subjects atremble
when Arlene brays like livestock
her 'blood-red lines' presage red lines of blood
(I historify) I sing
earworm Bo into nursery rhyme renown
crashing him from a peace wall the wrong side
if Bo cannot unknot her No who
cannot not exit Brexit or
I'll seek my self to not live in his state
uncrown my subjection as citizen of Scotland

4

I could sing you a list
from livid experience embedded
embattled Brexit furies
the scourge of Brussels
'taking out' Northern Ireland
for a Freeport
getting Brexit done (with)
back bench thumbs thumping 'no'
on backlit screens to Twitter
I could sign you a letter
with meaningful votes unvoided of meaning
no death row deal for Last Hope Island
I could sign my own name *here* at last
where Milton scribbled his Hancock

5

stuck-up *Stella* or dieting *Diana*
delicious *Delia* with her bland blandishments
muses invading the Brexit grove snagged
on tricky rhymes floored by bloated gimmicks
I sing them all no technician of thought I
make songs think and think in song new
thoughts new ways new times regarded
let's not slag off my sisters-in-sonnets
even the electorate may speak of the elect
Bo's anthem is now a one-note-samba
his target is near his aim is far each
little motion in Parliament felled
his deal agreed but amendments paused
once chaos choruses my song collapses

6

I saw the Cum hop like a frog
into the PM's car
a little fitting jig to jog
the EU's Flexibrexnextension
off the party playlist
affective policy
pulses through this poem
panting desire quivers against this mean time
my trembling legs enwrap my stateless love
my screaming delight
descants on my descent
into the dissenting life of passion
unzip this Halloween dead ditch Brexit catsuit
and let my dancing pussy out

7

50 years ago 'we'
reached the moon which still
looks down on us at night
in deepest sleep
blinking blind I dream
of writing *To the Moone*
but the cosmology's wrong
(like that Brexit Party candidate's
who claims to come from
Sirius) gross mother
of deep melancholy cool
tears are for the earth now
my fierce thought hots up under
the influence of moonshine

8

motor of this globalised world
in its entropic cosmos
human orrery I
drop down the plughole
dye my hair with a plastic bag
on my head pour
unguents for my wrinkled patches
my mirrored dark eyes blur
starry fantasy
Corbyn scorches among
his prime movers
praised in his idea's orbit
Bo bursts bleary from the PM's car
to lay a wreath upside down

9

she kept Bo's secrets (which
ones?) been his 'friend'
(she says) his faith his love
of self short term shelf
election promises or flood mop
photo op
flies to him zero halo'd number 1
0 above his crop of deceit where he
may breach his bond *There*
are bigger things at stake
hidden Russian bots beyond right
and wrong while the twisting
coward gifts 'relatable' jokes
My Fuckbox just exploded!

10

Big Chief of ampledom's
entire and perfect UK Fat
Cheque deal gifting ermine
to Brexipeers the paedo's
royal mint 'beyond reproach'
he head butts cackling truths
Muse you're tasked to sing now
speak differently don't debate Fact
Check his praise his spending
his powers temper his banal self
interest as 'Sweet lady' he calls
'drench me in your golden showers' soon
he'll rage 'Let age sit on your face'
and slam the hotline down

11

it's only me my mind
pressing a few words into
the politics of kindness as
Labour releases its Leavers
with counterclaims to claims
of Bo's retreat from zealous trade talk
what should command his truth and
election probity is in truth probed
by his high command each bounty
the Cum bids to our attention don't
stand dumb like a trussed chicken
awaiting its chlorine Trump rub
trust yourself to say you are only you
but to the rest say *you are many* …

12

human hair strung on a banjo un-
mute cameras catch subject
formations fiddling one tune while
another burns the world the two-faced fan
of Brexit eyeballs Erdoğan creeping by Bo
in NATO impotence no Euro-Muse
sings the fame of Trump his un-
conscious is a high strung blackbox plinkety-plink
I'm as perfect as Drayton's muse dictates
chorused goddess of these verses I'll
cause *my* cause to survive if he elects me
at post-election dawn as speaker of his house
of words for my heart blows imperfect power
beyond the trumpet of all fame

13

normal rules do not
apply rituals of public mourning
ennoble Bo's agendas of hate all I
have is a vote
to loosen the lies in the street my
simple name belies alluring flashes
on my secret shades my rippling breasts
bury the poet's voice since
the BBC can't swing it my public
service clarity invites Ice-Block Bo
to perform and prove his promises
at his no-show I empty-line him
[   ]
still they praise his invisible light

uncrown my beauty
my sunshine face (and all
the rest) I know I'm drowning
in traumatic realism post-election
sing Big Idea on her ideas gazes
knows she's Brexpiring
in the heat of Bo's pearly spume
at the nectarean fountain of his
vanity techno-dogging site
destiny's divinity 'got done'
dying laughs a last laugh leaving
I'm transfigured into a bigger idea
shifting an imaginary where I'll
remain for all eyes to behold

Selected Resources

Bate, Jonathan, *Soul of the Age: The Life, Mind and World of William Shakespeare*. London: Penguin, 2009.

Braidotti, Rosi. *Nomadic Theory: The Portable Rosi Braidotti*. New York: Columbia University Press, 2011.

Brett, Cyril (ed.). *Minor Poems of Michael Drayton* (Oxford: the Clarendon Press, 1907), available online at gutenbergorgfiles/17873/17873-h/17873-h.htm#Page_1.

Brink, Jean R. *Michael Drayton Revisited*. Boston: Twayne, 1990.

Capp, Bernard. 'The Poet and the Bawdy Court: Michael Drayton and the Lodging-House World in Early Stuart London.' *Seventeenth Century* 10 (1995): 27–37.

Dickens, Charles. 'The Boy at Mugby', in *The Signalman*. London: Profile Books, 2015.

Drayton, Michael, 'To Idea' in *Endimion and Phoebe, Ideas Latmvs*, entered into the Stationers' Register, April 1594, online at luminarium.org/renascence-editions/ren.htm.

Drayton, Michael. 'Idea.' in Arundell Esdaile, ed. *Daniel's Delia and Drayton's Idea*. London: Chatto and Windus: 1908. 67-141; online at Luminarium: luminarium.org/editions/idea.htm.

Evans, Maurice, ed. Revised by Roy J. Booth. *Eizabethan Sonnets*. London and North Clarendon: Phoenix Paperback, 2003.

Guattari, Félix. *The Three Ecologies*. London and New Brunswick: The Athlone Press, 2000.

Nicholl, Charles. *The Lodger: Shakespeare on Silver Street*. London: Penguin, 2008.

Tuley, Mark. ed. *Elizabethan Sonnet Cycles: Five Major Elizabethan Sonnet Cycles: by Samuel Daniel, Michael Drayton, Sir Philip Sidney, William Shakespeare and Edmund Spenser*. Maidstone: Kent Crescent Moon Publishing, 2010.

Jamie Toy, 'Moving But Staying the Same Crisis, Poetry and the Temporality of Brexit,' in *Versopolis* : versopolis.com/arts to-read /792/moving-but-also-staying-the-same, June 2019.

Wood, James. 'Diary, *London Review of Books*, 4th July 2019: 36-7.

Note

Michael Drayton's 1619 edition of *Idea*, which 'Bad Idea' transposes, may be read entire in Evans and Tuley.

Index to 'Idea's Mirror': dates of composition and sources in the editions of Michael Drayton's sonnets:

1: 8th October 2019; 1605: Sonnet 57

2: 15th October 2019; 1605: To Sir Walter Aston, Knight of the honourable order of the Bath, and my most worthy Patron

3: 17th October 2019: 1602: Sonnet 63 (To the high and mighty Prince, James, King of Scots)

4: 20th October 2019: 1599: Sonet 1

5: 24th October 2019: 1599: Sonet 3 (printed as prologue here)

6: 30th October (one day short of Brexit Day 2, Halloween) 2019:1599: Sonet 9

7: 5th November 2019: 1599: Sonet 11 (To the Moone)

8: 11th November 2019: 1599: Sonet 23 (To the Spheares)

9: 18th November 2019: 1599: Sonet 27

10: 21ˢᵗ November 2019: 1599: Sonet 57 (To the Excellent and most accomplisht Ladie: *Lucie* Countesse of Bedford); incorporating a phrase from the Eighth Eclogue of *Poemes lyrick and pastorall* (1606)

11: 28ᵗʰ November 2019: 1599: Sonet 58 (*To the Lady* Anne Harington)

12: 5ᵗʰ December 2019: *Ideas Mirrour* 1594: Amour 4

13: 9ᵗʰ December 2019: *Ideas Mirrour* 1594: Amour 5

14: 15ᵗʰ December 2019: *Ideas Mirrour* 1594: Amour 9

These 14 poems by Drayton may be found online at robertsheppard. blogspot.com/2019/12/michael-drayton-and-my-borrowings-from html

Bad Idea forms the second book of a trilogy *The English Strain.* Part one is entitled *The English Strain;* parts have been published as *Petrarch 3* (Crater Press), and *Hap: Understudies of Thomas Wyatt's Petrarch* (Knives, Forks and Spoons), and is published as *The English Strain* (Shearsman). The third part of the project is called *British Standards.*

www.ingramcontent.com/pod-product-compliance
Lightning Source LLC
Chambersburg PA
CBHW071236090426
42736CB00014B/3100